Original title:
A Frosted Whisper

Copyright © 2024 Swan Charm
All rights reserved.

Author: Paula Raudsepp
ISBN HARDBACK: 978-9916-79-459-3
ISBN PAPERBACK: 978-9916-79-460-9
ISBN EBOOK: 978-9916-79-461-6

Chill in the Air

The breeze whispers low,
Carrying secrets,
Of nights bathed in frost,
And stars that glow.

The trees stand so still,
Wrapped in a shroud,
Nature breathes softly,
With winter's will.

Each breath leaves a trace,
A mist in the night,
Fingers of ice reach,
For warmth in the space.

Footsteps crunch lightly,
On pathways of white,
Hushed moments linger,
Until dawn's first light.

A chill in the air,
Awakens pure hope,
For spring will return,
With love's gentle flare.

Secrets in the Snow

Gentle flakes descend,
Covering the ground,
In silence they fall,
A blanket profound.

Whispers in the night,
Each flake tells a tale,
Hidden in the soft,
Silent, pale veil.

Memories buried deep,
Yearning to be found,
In the quiet world,
Of white all around.

The moonlight dances bright,
On the frosty glow,
Unveiling the dreams,
Held close in the snow.

With every soft step,
A promise is made,
To cherish the beauty,
That will never fade.

Silences of Winter

Stillness wraps the earth,
In a frosty embrace,
Lost in the whispers,
Of winter's soft grace.

Clouds hang like dreams,
Overcast and gray,
Silence holds the air,
In a delicate sway.

Stars hide shyly now,
Behind layers of white,
The world seems paused,
In the calm of the night.

Branches bare and strong,
Reach out for the sky,
In the quiet's hold,
As time drifts by.

Within the stillness,
Lies a heart that beats,
For spring's warm return,
And its gentle retreats.

The Hushed Embrace of Cold

A kiss from the frost,
Fingers brush the ground,
In twilight's soft grip,
The world makes no sound.

Each breath fills the air,
With clouds of soft white,
As shadows creep in,
To embrace the night.

Snow blankets the earth,
With stories untold,
Whispers of the wind,
In the heart of the cold.

The glow of the moon,
Casts magic around,
In the hush of this time,
A peace can be found.

Holding all its dreams,
In a starry sweep,
The cold wraps us close,
As the world falls asleep.

Veils of Ice and Echo

Veils of ice hang low,
Whispers of the frost,
Silent shadows dance,
In the moonlight lost.

Echoes through the trees,
Crisp and sharp they ring,
Nature holds her breath,
In the cold, we cling.

Footprints mark the path,
Glittering like stars,
Every step a song,
Written in memoirs.

A chill wraps around,
Crystals in a song,
Timeless winter's hold,
Where all dreams belong.

Beneath the silver glow,
The night's embrace so tight,
Veils of ice and echo,
Shimmer in the night.

Frigid Tales on the Wind

Frigid tales unwind,
Carried by the breeze,
Stories of the frost,
That whisper through the trees.

The chill wraps the earth,
In shrouds of white attire,
Branches bow in grace,
While hearts blaze like fire.

Cold fingers of dusk,
Reach down to embrace,
Each tale softly spun,
In the winter's face.

Snowflakes swirl and twirl,
Like dancers in the night,
Tracing frigid paths,
Vital, pure, and bright.

With every breath we take,
The wind will softly call,
Frigid tales of wonder,
An echo to us all.

A Choreography of Cold

A choreography,
Performed on the snow,
Nature's quiet steps,
In the twilight glow.

Winter's breath so soft,
Caresses the land,
Each movement a gift,
By a gentle hand.

Frosted lace appears,
On branches like a crown,
Graceful in the chill,
In a world renowned.

Whirling flurries spin,
Carving paths anew,
In this icy dance,
Life begins to brew.

With every soft sigh,
The silence unfolds,
A choreography of cold,
In the winter's holds.

Ripples in a Frosted Silence

Ripples in silence,
Drawn through icy streams,
Midnight's cool embrace,
Where the starlight gleams.

Each flake a whisper,
Soft as a sigh,
Unraveling the dark,
As time wanders by.

Frosted breath hangs low,
In the still air's grace,
Echoes of the past,
In this tranquil space.

Muffled steps echo,
A dance of unseen souls,
In the frost-kissed night,
Where the story unfolds.

Ripples in a hush,
Gentle as a kiss,
Frosted silence speaks,
In the night, pure bliss.

In the Grip of Winter's Tune

Whispers of frost wrap the trees,
The world sleeps under blankets of white.
Stars twinkle like icy dreams,
In winter's embrace, the night feels bright.

Shadows dance in moonlit gleam,
Footsteps crunch on the frozen ground.
Echoes of laughter blend with the stream,
In silence, a soothing peace is found.

The chill bites but the heart feels warm,
Hot cocoa warms eager hands.
Each flake tells a tale of charm,
With winter's grace, the world expands.

The wind carries secrets untold,
As branches sway, life takes a rest.
In the grip of cold, warmth unfolds,
Finding joy in each snow-laden nest.

Nature whispers, tender and light,
Under the stars, our dreams take flight.
With every breath, winter's perfume,
We find solace in winter's tune.

Footprints in a Frozen World

Footprints trace a quiet path,
In a world draped in silver sheen.
Each step whispers the aftermath,
Of moments lost, yet serene.

Beneath a sky of muted gray,
The silence sings of winter's grace.
Every step a soft ballet,
Leaving marks in the snow's embrace.

Warmth emerges from within,
As stories linger with the chill.
A journey starts, where souls begin,
Through winter's grasp, we climb the hill.

Glistening trails weave stories old,
Echoing laughter along the way.
In the frozen land, tales unfold,
With every breath, we choose to stay.

Amidst the cold, connections grow,
As we walk in the night's bright swirl.
Footprints leading to tomorrow's glow,
In the beauty of a frozen world.

The Soft Tread of Frosted Trails

In the stillness, frost unfolds,
Nature wears a shimmered shawl.
The landscape whispers classic tales,
Of winter's hold and its icy thrall.

Every step we take, so light,
The snow like whispers underfoot.
Paths appear in the fading light,
While shadows dance where dreams take root.

Silent woods embrace the night,
The moon casts shadows deep and long.
With every breath, hearts feel the light,
In frosted trails, we find our song.

Stars pepper the dark canvas wide,
Guiding us through the icy air.
With every turn, we find a guide,
The soft tread leads us without care.

Awake in winter's mellow sound,
With each footfall, stories combine.
In frosted trails, love can be found,
As we wander through this design.

Echoes of a Snowbound Heart

In the hush of falling flakes,
The world slows down and listens near.
Every breath, a longing ache,
Echoes of love linger clear.

Snowflakes dance on the eager breeze,
Painting the earth in hues of calm.
Whispers carried through the trees,
In winter's heart, we find our balm.

A fire flickers, shadows play,
Warmth wrapped in a blanket's hold.
Outside, the cold steals day,
But within, stories are softly told.

In silence spun from winter's thread,
Each heartbeat matches nature's flow.
In this stillness, words unsaid,
Become the warmth of love's soft glow.

As night settles, deep and bright,
The world transformed, aglow with art.
In the frost, we find the light,
Echoes found in a snowbound heart.

Veils of Shimmering Dreams

In twilight's glow, where visions play,
Soft echoes dance, in hues of gray.
A tapestry weaves, from dusk to dawn,
Threads of hope, in the light drawn.

Whispers of stars, in the velvet night,
Carry the dreams, of lovers' flight.
Through silken paths, we gently glide,
With every breath, the worlds collide.

Floating on clouds, of shimmering light,
We chase the shadows, avoiding the fright.
In the embrace of magic's grace,
We find our way, to a sacred place.

With every heartbeat, the colors blend,
Creating a narrative, without an end.
In the mirror of fate, we softly gaze,
Finding our truths, in the cosmic haze.

So linger awhile, in this dreamy scheme,
Where life is but a wondrous dream.
As the veils lift, and secrets gleam,
We dance forever, in shimmering streams.

The Cool Caress of a Soft Whisper

A breeze flows softly, through willow's leaves,
Caressing shadows, where heart believes.
In murmured tones, the night reveals,
The tender thoughts that time conceals.

Moonlight drapes, on a silver sea,
As echoing sighs, drift back to me.
Each fleeting moment, a secret shared,
In the cool caress, we're gently bared.

Through the silence, words find their way,
Like leaves that tumble, come what may.
In hidden corners, our souls entwine,
The softest whispers, forever align.

As daylight breaks, and shadows fade,
Memories linger, as dreams cascade.
Every sigh, a promise holds,
In the cool caress, where love unfolds.

So listen closely, let silence speak,
In whispered grace, find what we seek.
The heart's soft calling, a tune so sweet,
In the moment of stillness, we are complete.

Twinkling Silence

Stars whisper softly in the night,
Dreams dance, caught in silver light.
A hush blankets the world below,
In twinkling silence, secrets flow.

Moonbeams drip on the sleeping trees,
Gentle winds carry heartfelt pleas.
Every shadow holds a tale untold,
In a tranquil embrace, the night unfolds.

Echoes of laughter from days long past,
In quiet moments, memories cast.
Breaths of the cosmos fill the air,
Twinkling silence, beyond compare.

The midnight sky, a canvas vast,
Painted with moments that zip by fast.
Time stands still in this sacred space,
In twinkling silence, we find our place.

As dawn approaches, the stars shall fade,
Yet, in our hearts, their light is laid.
Forever cherished, they'll always shine,
In twinkling silence, love intertwines.

Breath of the Winter Spirit

Whispers of frost in the crisp, cold air,
Nature's breath paints the world with care.
Trees don cloaks of purest white,
In winter's grasp, the land ignites.

Glistening crystals on the ground,
Every step makes a gentle sound.
The chill wraps around, a soft embrace,
As time slows down in this sacred place.

Beneath the stars, the quiet spreads,
A blanket of peace where the spirit treads.
The moon watches over, a guardian bright,
Guiding lost souls through the long, dark night.

With every gust, the whispers rise,
Crafting stories beneath the skies.
Nature breathes, a timeless song,
The winter spirit, hearty and strong.

As the dawn breaks, warm rays will gleam,
But in this moment, we hold the dream.
With breath of winter, we find our way,
In a world transformed, come what may.

Murmurs in the Chill

The night air hums with a muted sound,
Murmurs in the chill of the frosty ground.
Each breeze carries secrets old and wise,
A symphony played under starlit skies.

Shadows stretch long, their stories breathe,
In whispered tones, the night they weave.
A solitude profound cloaks the earth,
In the shadows, echoes find their worth.

Footsteps crunch on a frosted path,
With each step taken, the silence laughs.
Nature's lullaby wraps tight and close,
In the embrace of night, we become engrossed.

Cold air swirls like a ghostly dance,
In twilight's glow, we lose our stance.
Murmurs of winter beckon us near,
In the chill of the night, we conquer our fear.

As dawn beckons with a warming light,
We carry the murmurs from the night.
Memories linger in the crisp, still air,
In every breath, the chill we share.

Silvered Shadows

In twilight's glow, shadows come alive,
Silvered edges where dreams contrive.
Each corner holds a story untold,
In silvered shadows, mysteries unfold.

Moonlit paths where the heart dares roam,
Familiar places feel like home.
Beneath the stars, secrets intertwine,
In the dance of the night, all stars align.

Soft whispers brush against the skin,
The world pauses, a hush within.
Stars ignite in the deep, dark skies,
While silvered shadows conceal our sighs.

Moments linger in the cool night air,
Carried softly, without a care.
Light and darkness together the play,
In silvered shadows, we find our way.

As dawn threatens with colors bright,
Silver turns to gold in morning light.
Yet in the heart, those shadows remain,
In silvered whispers, we embrace the pain.

Frosty Threads of Gossamer

Softly spun in silver light,
Frosty threads weave through the night.
Nature's quilt, a whispered grace,
Cloaks the earth in cool embrace.

Crystal beads on branches sway,
Dancing gently, bright and gay.
Each glimmer sparkles, pure and true,
A tapestry the moon outgrew.

Gossamer dreams on frosted ground,
Whispers echo all around.
Captured stillness in the air,
Fragrant breath of winter's care.

Whispers Dancing on Winter's Edge

Whispers soft upon the breeze,
Echoing through frosted trees.
Winter's edge, a silent song,
Where the shadows stretch and long.

Crimson hues paint the twilight,
Holding on to fading light.
Dancing flakes, a fleeting waltz,
In the stillness, nature calls.

Footsteps crunching, crisp and clear,
Every sound brings winter near.
In the hush, a secret spun,
Whispers dancing, day is done.

Harmonies of Frozen Stillness

In the grove where silence reigns,
Frozen stillness, nature's chains.
Harmonies of ice and air,
In this quiet, hearts laid bare.

Every flake, a note divine,
Crafting echoes, pure, benign.
Nature sings in gentle tones,
A symphony that chills the bones.

Beneath the snow, life breathes anew,
In the hush, a hope so true.
Frozen stillness, timeless pause,
A winter's breath, a silent cause.

The Hushed Cry of a Pale Dawn

The dawn awakes, a hush in sight,
Pale and tender, soft as light.
In the morning's gentle grace,
Nature stirs, a slow embrace.

Clouds like whispers linger low,
Painting skies with hues that glow.
Every shadow, every ray,
Tells the tale of night's decay.

Frozen fingers on the grass,
In this moment, seasons pass.
The hush carries, sweet and calm,
A pale dawn, the world's balm.

Frigid Footprints

In the frost of winter's breath,
Footprints linger, cold in depth,
Each step whispers tales of old,
A silent journey, brave and bold.

Crisp air drapes the land in white,
Nature garbed in pure delight,
Shadows dance around the trees,
With every gust, they bend and freeze.

Beneath the sky, so vast and gray,
We wander freely, night or day,
The crunch of snow beneath our feet,
A melody, both soft and sweet.

Hushed conversations, nature's tune,
As winter sings beneath the moon,
Frigid footprints, a fleeting trace,
Of wandering souls that time can't erase.

So let us roam where few have tread,
Through frozen paths, where stories spread,
In each imprint, a memory formed,
In frigid footprints, warmth still warmed.

Luminescent Silence

In the stillness of the night,
Stars emerge, a gentle light,
Moonbeams weave their silver thread,
In luminescent silence, we're led.

Crickets sing their soft refrain,
While shadows dance, unbound by chain,
Whispers float on velvet air,
A sacred bond, a beauty rare.

Hearts beat softly, intertwined,
In this stillness, peace we find,
Time extends, as moments blend,
In luminescent silence, we mend.

Dreams take flight, like fleeting sighs,
Touched by magic, we realize,
Underneath the cosmic dome,
In this quietude, we roam.

So let us linger, hand in hand,
In this soft, enchanted land,
Where light and silence softly play,
In luminescent silence, we stay.

Veil of the Icy Dawn

Morning breaks with a chill embrace,
A veil of frost, a tranquil space,
Sunrise glimmers on frozen streams,
Whispers of warmth in waking dreams.

Beneath the silence, life awaits,
Nature stirs at dawn's bright gates,
Birdsongs break the icy calm,
A melody, a soothing balm.

Each fragile crystal, each hushed sigh,
Reflects the glow of waking sky,
Veil of the morn, so pure and bright,
Cloaked in beauty, kissed by light.

As shadows fade and colors blend,
The day begins, a journey penned,
In every twinkle, hope reborn,
In the veil of the icy dawn.

So let us greet what lies ahead,
With hearts wide open, fears shed,
For in this moment, we are drawn,
To the promise of the icy dawn.

Whispers Beneath the Snow

Underneath the blanket white,
Stories lie, tucked out of sight,
Softly sleeping, dreams unfold,
Whispers in the air, untold.

Winter's hush, a gentle sigh,
As flakes descend from twilight sky,
A tapestry of tales we weave,
In the silence, we believe.

Footsteps fade, but echoes last,
Memories of the seasons past,
Within the snow, a magic flows,
What lies hidden, only snow knows.

Nature's quilt, a woven thread,
Beneath its weight, all fears are shed,
With hearts aglow, we walk in peace,
In whispers deep, our souls find ease.

So let us pause, breathe in the chill,
Listen close, and feel the thrill,
For beneath the peaceful glow,
Are whispers sweet beneath the snow.

Chill of Silent Echoes

In the night where shadows creep,
Whispers of the past, they seep.
Silent echoes gently roam,
Melodies that lead me home.

In the air, a frozen sigh,
Underneath the moonlit sky.
A haunting tune, a fleeting glance,
Frozen moments in a dance.

Nights exchanged for days of light,
Echoes speak in soft respite.
Memories wrapped in silver sheen,
Fleeting glimpses of what has been.

Through the mist, I wander lost,
Counting every dream and cost.
Time slips through my open hands,
As silent echoes weave their strands.

In the chill, a heart exposed,
Each surrender deeply throes.
Yet within this quiet plight,
Hope will dawn with morning light.

Crystal Veins of Memory

Fractured dreams in glimmered glass,
Fleeting moments come to pass.
With each shard, a story told,
In reflections, life unfolds.

Veins of crystal, bright and clear,
Whisper secrets held so dear.
Memories sparkle in the night,
Painting shadows, soft and bright.

Every drop a fleeting grace,
Cascading in this fragile space.
Hold them close, do not forget,
In their luster, no regret.

In the silence, echoes play,
Time stands still, then slips away.
Fragments woven, dreams entwined,
In crystal veins, our hearts aligned.

Glimmers fade, but still they gleam,
Fleeting is the heart's sweet dream.
Yet in twilight's gentle glow,
Crystal veins of love still flow.

Frost-Kissed Dreams

Whispers danced on morning air,
Chilled by whispers, we beware.
Frosty tendrils touch the night,
Turning dreams to icy light.

Footprints fade on snow-white ground,
In the stillness, hope is found.
Every breath a misty swirl,
As the dreams begin to unfurl.

In the quiet, hearts beat soft,
Crystallized, our thoughts float aloft.
Winter wraps its arms around,
Cradling the lost dreams we've found.

Stars reflected on the snow,
Frost-kissed dreams no longer glow.
Yet deep inside, a fire burns,
Through the cold, the heart still yearns.

Let the frosty winds then weave,
Stories of what we believe.
In the chill, we find our way,
Frost-kissed dreams that never fray.

The Shiver of Lost Time

Fleeting moments, shadows cast,
Echoes of a distant past.
In the twilight, memories chime,
Speaking softly of lost time.

Glimmers fade like wisps of air,
What was once so bright, now bare.
In the silence, time stands still,
Yet the heart holds on, with will.

Every heartbeat, every sigh,
A reminder as hours fly.
Fingers grasp at what remains,
In the shiver, love explains.

Ghostly figures walk the line,
Through the shadows, lost in time.
Yet within each shivering breath,
Lies a whisper, conquering death.

Let the winds of change entwine,
Embers glowing through the pine.
In the dusk, we find our rhyme,
In the shiver of lost time.

Whispering through Icy Veils

Whispers dance on frosty air,
Silence cloaked in frozen flare.
Each flake holds a tale to tell,
In the hush, where shadows dwell.

Moonlight kisses snowy ground,
In the stillness, dreams are found.
Beneath the veils of winter's art,
Echoes play, they tug the heart.

Branches bow with crystals bright,
Nature's jewels in soft twilight.
Secrets linger, cool and deep,
In the silence, memories sleep.

Footsteps crunch on powdery snow,
Paths of wanderers long ago.
Each step whispers, each breath sighs,
Underneath the starry skies.

The night will hold these secrets near,
In frost and calm, there's nothing to fear.
For in this world, so bold yet frail,
We find our peace, through icy veils.

Crystalline Reverie

In a world of silver sheen,
Every flake a vibrant dream.
Glimmers dancing in the night,
Nature's canvas, pure delight.

Underneath the moon's embrace,
Shadows weave through time and space.
Infinite patterns, crisp and bright,
Whirling softly in the light.

Frosted whispers gently call,
Echoes softly rise and fall.
In this moment, lost in peace,
Winter's magic will not cease.

Dreams unfold in layers white,
Crystalline wonders, sheer delight.
Each breath taken, sharp and clear,
In this reverie, winter's near.

As the dawn begins to break,
Winter's touch will softly wake.
Yet in dreams of crisp repose,
Crystalline beauty still bestows.

Secrets in the Snow

Snowflakes fall, a hush prevails,
Shrouded whispers tell their tales.
Softly landing, pure and light,
Secrets held in winter's night.

Frozen branches, silent screens,
Hidden stories, whispered dreams.
Beneath the surface, truth remains,
Cloaked in white, the world contains.

In the stillness, hear the call,
Nature's breath, a gentle thrall.
Every flake a lost embrace,
Touch the heart, a fleeting trace.

Footprints mark a path unknown,
In the snow, our thoughts are sown.
Each adventure, shimmering light,
Leads to warmth in winter's night.

Out in the cold, but not alone,
With every secret, love is shown.
In the snow, beneath the glow,
We find our hearts, where secrets flow.

The Breath of Winter's Muse

Breath of winter, crisp and bright,
Shimmers softly in the light.
In the silence, dreams take flight,
Wrapped in magic, pure delight.

Whispers glide on frosty air,
Nature's canvas, truth laid bare.
With each sigh, the world transforms,
In frozen beauty, life conforms.

Footsteps echo through the trees,
Carried gently by the breeze.
In this moment, time stands still,
Winter's grace, a tranquil thrill.

Stars above in velvet night,
Sparkle with a silver light.
Every breath, a treasured muse,
In winter's grasp, our souls diffuse.

As dawn breaks with a tender glow,
Winter's magic starts to slow.
Yet in each breath, a sweet reprise,
The muse lives on in icy skies.

The Language of Frost

Whispers dance on silver panes,
Each breath a world of icy chains.
Silent tales of winter's art,
Frosted words that chill the heart.

Night's embrace, a quiet shroud,
Under stars, the sky so proud.
Nature speaks in cold delight,
In every flake that falls at night.

Branches lace in silver hues,
Frozen lakes reflect the blues.
Footsteps soft on snowy ground,
Echoes of a world unbound.

Crystal crowns on every tree,
A symphony of frosty glee.
Voices carried by the breeze,
Weaving tales among the trees.

In the stillness, magic flows,
A language only winter knows.
Each fleeting moment, pure and fast,
The language of frost, forever cast.

Icy Murmurs

Beneath the veil of frosted breath,
Whispers weave through winter's death.
Softly spoken, tales of old,
In icy murmurs, secrets told.

Crystals form in twilight's glow,
Glistening paths where silence flows.
Every flake a story spun,
In the dance of dusk, we run.

Nature sighs in frosty night,
Twinkling stars, a distant light.
Rustling leaves in chilly air,
Icy murmurs, soft as prayer.

Footprints pressed in snow so deep,
Memory's echo starts to creep.
Each whisper holds a lingering thought,
In the stillness, battles fought.

A hush descends, the world takes pause,
In winter's breath, we find our cause.
Icy murmurs, soft and clear,
In their embrace, we draw near.

A Haunting Frost

In the gray of morning light,
Frost clings softly, a chilling sight.
Echoes fade where shadows creep,
A haunting frost, a slumber deep.

Glistening whispers in the air,
Nature draped in frosty prayer.
Softly sighs the waking land,
A frozen world, unplanned and grand.

Crystal formations catch the sun,
Every shard, a story spun.
In the silence, memories roar,
A haunting frost, forevermore.

Wandering through this icy haze,
The heart calls out in winter's maze.
With every step, the cold confides,
In haunting frost, the spirit glides.

As day breaks through this chilly veil,
Winter's magic will prevail.
With every breath, a chill remains,
In haunting frost, the soul still gains.

Gentle Crystals

Gentle crystals fall like dreams,
Whispering of soft moonbeams.
Twirling down in playful flight,
Transforming day into night.

A quilt of white upon the ground,
Where silent wonders can be found.
Every flake a fleeting kiss,
In gentle crystals, we find bliss.

With open arms, the world awaits,
As nature weaves its magic fates.
Children laugh in pure delight,
Chasing crystals, hearts take flight.

Underneath the winter skies,
Gentle crystals, sweet surprise.
A moment's touch, a fleeting grace,
In frozen magic, we embrace.

As twilight drapes the earth anew,
Gentle whispers beckon through.
In every flake, a story swirls,
Gentle crystals, winter's pearls.

Flickers of Ice-Kissed Remembrance

In twilight's glow, a whisper calls,
Forgotten dreams on frost-clad walls.
Glimmers of laughter, pale and bright,
Dance like fireflies in the night.

Echoes linger in the still, cold air,
Silent secrets that we used to share.
With each step, a ghost from the past,
Fleeting moments, too sweet to last.

Winter's breath, a gentle sigh,
Beneath the stars, where memories lie.
Flickers of hope through the smothering chill,
A heart held captive, waiting still.

Frozen tresses of silver light,
Adorn the memories hidden from sight.
We chase the shadows, though they elude,
In the silence, our yearning is renewed.

Let the snowflakes weave their tales,
Through the night, as time unveils.
With every flake, a wish set free,
In the dance of ice, I find me.

The Gentle Tinge of Frozen Thoughts

Softly wraps the world around,
In winter's grasp, solace found.
Thoughts like snowflakes drift and sway,
Upon the breath of a fading day.

Gentle echoes of laughter remain,
Caught in the crystal, free from pain.
Threads of remembrance, warm and sweet,
Whispers dancing on frozen feet.

A sunbeam breaks, with golden thread,
Touching the dreams that we once fed.
Frozen smiles awaken anew,
Infused with warmth, in shades of blue.

Winds weave tales of the nightingale,
Melodies wrapped in a silvery veil.
Each note a spark, a flicker of grace,
In the stillness, our hearts embrace.

Through the frigid air, hopes take flight,
In the soft glow of fading light.
A gentle tinge of what once was,
Lingers on, like a whispered cause.

Shadows of Frost-Bitten Whispers

In the heart of winter's grasp we dwell,
Amidst the silence, stories to tell.
Frost-bitten whispers swirl and weave,
Tales of longing, memories leave.

The night wraps close, a shroud of dreams,
Shadows flicker, or so it seems.
In the stillness, time extends,
As echoes drift, the soul descends.

Moonlight spills on the pristine snow,
Guiding our thoughts where we dare to go.
Each soft footstep, a secret shared,
Entwined in silence, our hearts bared.

Glistened branches in twilight's haze,
Frame the moment in a frozen gaze.
Words unspoken yet clearly known,
In frost-kissed air, love has grown.

As shadows dance in the pale moon's light,
In silent harmony, hearts unite.
Whispers linger on winter's breath,
The whispers of life, amidst the death.

A Ballet of Ice and Silence

Under the stars, the world holds still,
A ballet blooms on the winter hill.
Frozen figures poised in grace,
In the quiet, we find our place.

Each movement soft, like falling snow,
In this realm, where whispers flow.
Twirling dreams, unchained and free,
A dance of ice, my soul and me.

Frost-kissed petals flutter near,
Sparkling jewels, crystal clear.
With every twirl, the hours fade,
In the silence, a serenade.

Moonlit shadows glide and sway,
Telling stories of yesterday.
In the still of night, time suspends,
A ballet that never ends.

Embraced by the cold, we spin anew,
In this dance, I find you.
Together we glide through soft, white mist,
A ballet of silence, sealed with a kiss.

Shivers of Serenity

In the hush of twilight's glow,
Whispers dance through the air,
Softly pulling shadows near,
Wrapped in calm, free from care.

Gentle waves of a fading light,
Crickets hum their sweet refrain,
Nature holds her breath tonight,
In this peace, there lies no pain.

Stars emerge like scattered dreams,
Flickering in velvet skies,
In the stillness, nothing seems
To disturb the night's soft sighs.

The world slows, a tender pause,
As the heart finds silent peace,
In the beauty of the cause,
Where all worries gently cease.

Embraced by the moonlit sea,
Soul and spirit intertwine,
In these shivers, there's a key,
To a joy that feels divine.

The Quiet Veil of January

January drapes the earth,
In a cloak of soft, white glaze,
Frosted whispers, hushed from mirth,
Underneath the winter's gaze.

Bare branches stretch across the sky,
Crystals hung where breezes chill,
Time slows down, as days pass by,
In the stillness, hearts can thrill.

Footsteps crunch on powdered snow,
Echoing where dreams take flight,
In the shadows, soft winds blow,
Guiding souls through endless night.

Each moment breathes in quiet grace,
Beneath a sky of muted tones,
Finding warmth in this still space,
Where the world lays down its bones.

January holds a secret tight,
Wrapped in silence, pure and deep,
In the quiet, find the light,
As the earth begins to sleep.

Fragments of Frost

Glistening on winter's breath,
Each fragment dances in delight,
Nature's canvas, a silent death,
In the depth of the crystal night.

A tapestry of icy lace,
Weaves through fields, serene and still,
Entranced, we wander, lost in space,
Nature's beauty, a wondrous thrill.

Every step, a tale untold,
Footprints lost in the purest white,
Stories born from the bitter cold,
In the shadows, echoes ignite.

Underneath the starry dome,
Fragments shimmer, a fleeting sight,
Inviting souls to wander home,
Through the whispers of the night.

In this gallery of the frozen,
Beauty hidden in each shard,
Where the seasons, softly chosen,
Gift us memories, never marred.

The Stillness of Snowfall

Snowflakes drift, a gentle fall,
Blanketing the world in white,
In this hush, I hear the call,
Of silence, holding day and night.

Each flake whispers secrets old,
As they twirl through the chilly air,
A tender story to be told,
In the stillness, none can compare.

Frozen moments, soft and rare,
Carpeted beneath nature's grace,
In the quiet, hearts laid bare,
Finding solace in this place.

Snowflakes fall like dreams that wane,
Falling softly, never stray,
In their descent, there's no pain,
Just a magic that holds sway.

The world transforms beneath their touch,
In this calm, we breathe so slow,
Caught in beauty's gentle clutch,
Feeling love in winter's glow.

Conversations Held in Snowlight

In whispers soft, the snowflakes fall,
Stars above, they shine and call.
Voices blend in winter's night,
Carried forth on beams of light.

Hushed secrets in the icy air,
Hearts converge in quiet prayer.
Each breath a cloud, so pure, so bright,
We find our dreams in snow's delight.

Footsteps crunch, a melody,
In this still world, we wander free.
Laughter dances, crisp and clear,
In the solace, we hold dear.

Time stands still, as snowflakes twirl,
Encased in warmth, our hearts unfurl.
The night listens to our tune,
Underneath the watchful moon.

The Stillness of Winter's Embrace

In winter's grasp, the world lies still,
Silent woods on frost-covered hill.
The breath of nature, cold and slow,
Wrapped in calm, the earth glows.

Branches bare, adorned with lace,
Time relinquished, in this space.
Every flake a whispered sigh,
Of seasons shifting, passing by.

The sky, a canvas, wide and grey,
Yet in the silence, new dreams play.
Moments linger, soft and bright,
In the warmth of winter's night.

A world transformed, serene, divine,
Where every heart can intertwine.
In stillness found, our spirits rise,
Beneath the blanket of snowy skies.

Serenity Wrapped in Snow

A tranquil hush, the snow descends,
With every flake, the silence lends.
Nature's quilt is laid with care,
In white embrace, we find our prayer.

Gentle breezes brush the trees,
Whispers dance with winter's freeze.
Moments caught in velvet light,
Wrapped in peace, our souls take flight.

The world, a portrait, calm and bright,
In frosty air, the heart feels right.
Snowflakes twirl on pathways white,
We wander through this pure delight.

Echoes of laughter, warm and clear,
In every heart, we hold so dear.
Serenity found in this glow,
As we bask in winter's snow.

The Trill of Frosty Frost

A trill awakens with the dawn,
Frosty whispers, gently drawn.
Nature's song, crisp and bright,
In the chill of morning light.

Branches shimmer, adorned in white,
The world aglow, a pure delight.
Birds take wing, their notes collide,
With the beauty winterside.

The air is filled with vibrant cheer,
Every echo, loud and clear.
In frosty breath, we find our way,
As winter weaves a bright display.

In crystal notes, the heart takes flight,
In every shard of purest light.
A melody of frost unfolds,
As the story of winter is told.

Quietude in Icebound Days

In the stillness, frost does gleam,
Beneath the sky, a silver beam.
Whispers echo, softly spread,
As nature sleeps upon its bed.

Icicles hang like silent tears,
Guarding secrets of past years.
Trees stand proud, adorned in white,
Cloaked in calm, serene delight.

Footprints dance on crystal ground,
In each crunch, a peaceful sound.
Breath of winter fills the air,
A moment's pause, a quiet prayer.

Fires crackle, shadows sway,
Cocoa warms on this cold day.
Books and blankets by the fire,
Winter's stillness, hearts inspire.

Time stands still in chilly grace,
Each heartbeat finds its rightful place.
In the icebound, peace is spun,
Quietude reigns, day is done.

Illuminated Silence

Moonlight dances on the lake,
Each ripple speaks but cannot wake.
Stars above, a gleaming choir,
Wrapped in darkness, dreams conspire.

Stillness weaves through every dream,
Thoughts drift softly, like a stream.
In this hush, a melody,
The heart finds calm, wild and free.

Echoes linger, fade away,
In the quiet, night holds sway.
Gentle whispers touch the soul,
In illuminated, peaceful whole.

In every shadow, hope takes flight,
Guided by the soft moonlight.
Each star a wish, each breath a hymn,
In silence, we learn not to skim.

Life slows down beneath the sky,
In this stillness, we find why.
Illuminated by the night,
Silence bends, all feels right.

The Tranquil Cry of Snowglobes

Inside the glass, a world is spun,
Whirling gently, a dance begun.
Snowflakes twirl in soft embrace,
Time stands still in this small space.

Each shake brings forth a winter's tale,
A fleeting glimpse where dreams set sail.
Figures frozen in joyful flight,
All captured in ethereal light.

Gentle melodies hum in the dome,
A peaceful symphony calls us home.
The tranquil cry, a soft refrain,
Evoking laughter, joy, and pain.

Children gaze with wide-eyed bliss,
In their wonder, they cannot miss.
The magic held within the glass,
A moment caught, like falling grass.

As seasons change, these scenes remain,
Whispers held in winter's chain.
The snowglobe's cry, so soft, so pure,
In fragile dreams, our hearts endure.

Echoes Beneath the Snow

Under layers white and deep,
Nature's secrets still do keep.
Beneath the hush, a world is stirred,
Silent voices, barely heard.

Branches creak with ancient tales,
Whispers ride the winter gales.
Echoes dance through icy trees,
Carried forth on chilly breeze.

Frozen ponds, a mirror's gaze,
Reflecting life in crystal haze.
Each flake a story, uniquely spun,
In winter's arms, all is one.

Footsteps weave through snowy lanes,
Echoes linger, soft remains.
In the quiet, thoughts unfold,
Beneath the snow, a joy untold.

In this stillness, hearts connect,
Nature's pulse, we all reflect.
Echoes beneath, so soft and light,
Hold us close on a winter's night.

Glistening Notes of Solitude

In the hush of night, stars gleam,
Their silver songs softly stream,
Whispers of peace linger here,
Amidst the silence, I hold dear.

Moonbeams cast shadows long,
In solitude, I find my song,
Each note a blend of joy and pain,
A melody danced in the rain.

Branches sway with gentle grace,
Embracing wind's warm embrace,
Nature's breath, a soothing balm,
In chaos, I find the calm.

Echoes in the stillness play,
Guiding dreams that drift away,
In moments brief, I stand alone,
In glistening notes, my heart has grown.

So let the night unravel slow,
In solitude, I've come to know,
Each whispered thought, a precious find,
Crafted softly in my mind.

Frigid Whispers of Twilight

As daylight fades, shadows creep,
Frigid whispers, secrets deep,
Twilight dances on the edge,
A silent, solemn, whispered pledge.

The chill wraps tight, a soft embrace,
In the waning light, I find my place,
Crimson skies, a fleeting glimpse,
Winter's breath in whispered hymns.

Stars awaken in the frost,
In their beauty, grief is lost,
They twinkle like forgotten dreams,
In the quiet, silence gleams.

Breath turns to mist, a fleeting sign,
In this twilight, worlds align,
Nature's heart, a thumping beat,
Frigid whispers, bittersweet.

The horizon holds a soft delight,
In the arms of approaching night,
With every step, I feel the chill,
A tranquil space where I can fill.

Veils of Snowlight

In the morning hush, snowflakes fall,
Creating veils that softly enthrall,
Each flake a whisper, pure and bright,
Wrapping the world in a cloak of white.

Footsteps echo in the deep,
Silent secrets the snow will keep,
Wonders born in the frosty glow,
As magic weaves through earth below.

The trees stand tall, adorned in lace,
Nature's art, a precious space,
Branches bow beneath the weight,
Of winter's kiss, both kind and great.

With every breath, I feel alive,
In this realm where dreams can thrive,
Veils of snowlight dancing near,
An endless promise, crystal clear.

So let me wander, lost in grace,
Through winter's maze, in this embrace,
Where beauty rests in purest form,
In veils of snowlight, I am warm.

The Fragile Dance of Frost

Upon the glass, the frost does weave,
A delicate tale, a heart reprieve,
Each crystal forming, shapes divine,
In morning's light, they softly shine.

A dance begins on winter's breath,
In whispered notes, it flirts with death,
The fragile lines, they twist and spin,
Creating beauty from within.

As I watch the patterns grow,
A fleeting art, a gentle show,
With every breath, the warmth collides,
And soon the frosted dance abides.

Yet in each line, a story told,
Of chilly nights, and moments bold,
Life's fragile dance, in time it fades,
Leaving only soft cascades.

So here I stand and watch the light,
Where frost and warmth share sweet delight,
In fragile dance, my heart can soar,
Embracing winter, forevermore.

Beneath the Frozen Surface

Under the ice, still waters glide,
Secrets of winter, frozen inside.
Whispers of nature, softly enclosed,
In the deep silence, time has dozed.

Drifting leaves, now locked in embrace,
Ghostly shadows, a hidden space.
Every motion, a story untold,
Crystals of memories, shimmering bold.

Icicles hang, like daggers of light,
A chill that compels the day to night.
Nature's heartbeat, slow and profound,
In the cold depths, mystery found.

Glancing upwards, the sky seems to cry,
Snowflakes descend, as dreams drift by.
Frozen reflections, floating and free,
Within the still waters, a world to see.

Time stands still, yet whispers away,
Beneath the surface, shadows play.
A realm untouched, bound by the frost,
In the still silence, all else is lost.

Glittering Stillness

Under the moon, the snowflakes gleam,
Each one a fragment, a delicate dream.
Stars above in the velvet sky,
Whispers of night, as shadows pass by.

Frozen branches, a crystalline lace,
In the quietude, we find our place.
With every breath, the world holds its sigh,
Wrapped in the beauty that cannot die.

Footprints linger where the silence speaks,
In stillness, the heart finds what it seeks.
Nature's canvas, painted in white,
Beneath the blanket of soft moonlight.

Gentle winds weave through the trees,
Carrying tales of the winter's freeze.
Each flake a story, a memory bold,
In the night's embrace, forever told.

Mirrored reflections upon the lake,
A dreamlike shimmer, the stillness awake.
In glittering quiet, harmony flows,
A tranquil moment, forever it grows.

Songs of Ice and Silence

Echoes of winter, a haunting refrain,
Songs from the ice, soft as the rain.
Beneath the surface, melodies swell,
In the stillness, ancient tales dwell.

Frost-kissed whispers, secrets abound,
Each note a memory, barely a sound.
Amidst the frozen, the heart starts to soar,
In the silence, we yearn for more.

Winds weave through branches, creating a tune,
Harmonies drifting beneath the pale moon.
With each gentle breath, the night begins,
A symphony woven as daylight thins.

Colors of ice dance in the light,
Reflecting the stories of day and night.
In crystalline beauty, we find our way,
Through music of silence, forever we stay.

Songs of the frozen, echo with grace,
In the heart of winter, we find our place.
Each note a promise, each lullaby sweet,
In the still of the night, our souls gently meet.

Captured in Cold

Icy hands grip a world so still,
Nature's embrace, a winter's chill.
Capturing moments, a lens made of frost,
In the quiet beauty, nothing is lost.

Each flake like a pearl, falling from grace,
Paints the landscape, a tranquil space.
Frozen horizons stretch far and wide,
In the depth of the cold, we find warmth inside.

Silent wonders in a white-draped scene,
Every corner, a magical sheen.
In the breath of the dawn, a soft glow appears,
Whispers of solace, melting the fears.

Captured in cold, our memories stay,
Each moment a treasure, day after day.
In the heart of the winter, we linger and dream,
As the world around us begins to gleam.

Holding the stillness, a moment so rare,
In the chill of the air, we find our care.
Letting time slip as we softly unfold,
In the essence of now, we're captured in cold.

Lullabies of Shimmering Chill

In twilight's glow, whispers weave,
A melody soft, where shadows cleave.
Stars twinkle bright, in velvet skies,
As night's embrace brings sweet lullabies.

Frosty fingers trace the moon,
Drawing dreams that softly croon.
Each breath of chill, a gentle sign,
In the hush, our hearts align.

Crystals dance on silver streams,
Casting spells on slumbered dreams.
The world is hushed, a sacred trance,
In shimmering night, we find our chance.

Snowflakes drift like softest sighs,
Painting the earth in whispered lies.
Each flake a tale, a secret told,
In the stillness, warm and cold.

So close your eyes, let worries cease,
In this moment, find your peace.
With lullabies that chill the night,
Embrace the dreams, let go of fright.

Chased by Winter's Branches

Through tangled boughs, the cold winds creep,
With icy fingers that nudge and sweep.
Shadows stretch as daylight fades,
Chasing warmth in twilight glades.

In the stillness, whispers call,
Echoes of seasons, rise and fall.
Branches bare against the gray,
A stark reminder of winter's sway.

Footfalls crunch on frost-kissed ground,
In solitude, a world unbound.
Each step leads deeper into cold,
A story of resilience told.

Clouds hover, heavy and low,
Painting the world in a pallid glow.
Yet in the silence, peace is found,
Chased by branches, we stand our ground.

So let the chill wrap us tight,
Embrace the dark, embrace the night.
For in the chase, we learn to see,
The beauty in winter's mystery.

Softest Touch of the Glacial Dawn

A gentle light breaks through the frost,
In glimmers soft, no warmth is lost.
Crystalline hues paint the morn,
Awakening life, the world is reborn.

Whispers of ice caress the air,
As nature stirs with tender care.
Each breath a cloud, a fleeting sign,
The dawn awakens, pure and divine.

Frost-edged flowers, bloom and bend,
In nature's grasp, a tale to send.
Silken threads in the sunlight's grace,
Invite the heart to find its place.

All around, the world breaths in,
Transforming silence where dreams begin.
The chill retreats, a soft embrace,
In glacial dawn, we find our space.

So let the light unveil the haze,
In the glacial dawn, we sing our praise.
With every heartbeat, softly spun,
We welcome life, a new day begun.

The Sentinels of Ice and Time

Amidst the stillness, sentinels rise,
Frozen guardians beneath the skies.
With icy crowns, they stand so tall,
A testament to the ages' call.

Each jagged edge tells tales untold,
Of seasons passed, both warm and cold.
Time's chisel marks the silent stone,
In icy whispers, we are not alone.

The winds howl tales of years gone by,
As snowflakes dance, and starlight sighs.
Cycles of life in their frozen frame,
Always changing, yet always the same.

Beneath the surface, life may dwell,
In hidden nooks, we cannot tell.
Sentinels watch with patient grace,
Time flows slowly in this hallowed space.

So heed the call of ice and stone,
In their presence, we are never alone.
For in their watch, our hearts will find,
The echoes of yesterday intertwined.

Voices of the Crystal Gale

Whispers ride the winter winds,
Through the trees, they dance and spin.
Echoes of tales left untold,
In the night, their wonders unfold.

Frozen breaths on my frozen skin,
Ghostly figures swirl within.
Chilling laughter fills the air,
As the frost bites everywhere.

Crystal notes glide through the dark,
Singing secrets, leaving a mark.
Every flake a soft-spoken song,
In the night, where they all belong.

Gales entwine like lovers' embrace,
Carving dreams in this sacred space.
Hush now, the symphony starts,
As the night mends our restless hearts.

Voices of the crystal gale,
Lead us softly, high and pale.
With every chill, I feel alive,
In this moment, we all thrive.

Shivering Shadows Beneath the Stars

Underneath a twilight sky,
Shadows ripple, weave, and sigh.
Gentle whispers fill the air,
With stories only night can share.

Stars twinkle like distant dreams,
Illuminating silver streams.
The moon casts light on silent trees,
Carried softly by the breeze.

Fingers trace the cosmic dance,
In the night, we take a chance.
Captured in the cool embrace,
Time unravels, we find our place.

Murmurs rise, a sweet dismay,
In the shadows, lost we stay.
Embracing fears, igniting hope,
In this twilight, we learn to cope.

Whispers linger, shadows sway,
Beneath this great celestial ballet.
Each moment woven like a thread,
In the light, we are gently led.

Dreams Carved in Snowflakes

Dancing softly on the breeze,
Snowflakes tumble, swirl with ease.
Crystal patterns fill the night,
Whispers of dreams, pure and bright.

Every flake a tale unveiled,
Silent secrets, softly hailed.
Fragile beauty, brief and rare,
In the twilight, they hang in air.

Caught in wonder, hearts aglow,
In this peaceful, silvery show.
Footprints fade upon the ground,
Echoing dreams that still resound.

In the hush, where magic grows,
Snowflakes speak in soft prose.
Gathering warmth, a gentle touch,
In their art, we find so much.

Carved in time, like whispering sighs,
Snowflakes fall from endless skies.
Dreams take flight with every flake,
In this world, we awake.

Lanterns of the Frosted Night

Lanterns glow with amber light,
Casting warmth on frostbit height.
Through the chill, they guide our way,
Shining bright, night turns to day.

Frosted air with magic swells,
In the light, where comfort dwells.
Every flicker tells a tale,
Of dreams that rise and never pale.

Footsteps trace the path of glow,
In the dark where whispers flow.
Lanterns sway like hearts that yearn,
For the warmth of love's return.

Through the quiet, we march on,
Guided by the coming dawn.
Hope ignites in every flame,
In the night, we're never the same.

Lanterns guard our secrets clear,
Holding dreams that draw us near.
In the frost, we find our light,
Together, we embrace the night.

Glimmering Thought in a Cold World

In shadows deep, a thought will spark,
A whisper clear, to light the dark.
Through icy winds and silent night,
A glimmer glows, a flickered light.

Amidst the chill, a warmth does rise,
Like stars that dance in velvet skies.
The heart discovers, though walls are tight,
A world reborn with each insight.

Fingers trace the frost on glass,
Connections bloom, as moments pass.
In every breath, a chance to see,
A tapestry of what could be.

The echoes fade, yet still persist,
A calling clear, too bright to miss.
In winter's grasp, the mind takes flight,
With glimmering thoughts, we find our light.

So let us wander, hand in hand,
Through frozen fields of drifted sand.
In glimmering thoughts, we'll pave the way,
To forge a path, come what may.

Cusp of Frosty Horizons

Upon the ridge where silence reigns,
A chilly breath through ripened grains.
The cusp of frost, a moment holds,
A story whispered, softly told.

The dawn unveils a glistening sheen,
As colors stretch, vibrant and keen.
Each horizon bears a mystic glow,
Awakening dreams we've yet to know.

Footprints left in snow so pure,
A path unseen, yet hearts endure.
With every step, the spirit glides,
Over frosty realms where wonder resides.

In stillness found, the world feels vast,
Chasing shadows of the past.
Yet in the cold, we find our voice,
Embracing life, we dare rejoice.

So stand with me, on winter's cusp,
As visions shimmer, hearts must trust.
With every breath, new worlds we find,
Together, weaving, heart and mind.

Traces of a Silenced Heart

In muted tones, a heart does weep,
Cloaked in shadows, secrets keep.
Yet whispers linger on the air,
Reminders soft of love laid bare.

Each trace a memory etched in time,
Like gentle waves, a silent chime.
In quiet moments, feelings rise,
Reflected softly in weary eyes.

The warmth of days, now faded dreams,
Still pulse with hope in fragile seams.
Through unshed tears, the heart rebuffs,
Within the silence lies the truths.

Though words may falter, hearts still sing,
In unison, the yearning brings.
For every sigh, a pressure mounts,
Fueling love's fire, our souls' accounts.

And in the dark, we'll find our way,
Through silenced hearts that still convey.
With traces left from love's sweet art,
We gather strength, though worlds apart.

The Breath of White Horizons

A breath of white, a world anew,
Where frost enfolds the earth in hue.
Each flake that falls whispers dreams,
In soft embrace, the spirit beams.

Horizons stretch in purest light,
An endless canvas, cold and bright.
Where time stands still, and silence reigns,
The heart finds peace amidst the strains.

Breath taken slow, a moment's grace,
In nature's arms, we find our place.
Amongst the pines, the whispers play,
An echo soft, guiding our way.

With every gust, new stories flow,
An ancient dance in winter's glow.
Aligning stars from far-off lands,
Uniting souls with unseen hands.

And in the chill of morning's wake,
Together, paths we dare to make.
The breath of white, our hearts embrace,
In frosty realms, we find our grace.

Whispered Secrets of the Snowdrifts

Beneath the blanket, whispers cling,
Softly cradled in winter's wing.
Frozen tales the moonlight weaves,
In snowdrifts where the quiet grieves.

Footsteps muffled, secrets fold,
Each flake a story yet untold.
The night wraps tight, a chilling sound,
In frozen realms where dreams are found.

Birches stand like ghostly guards,
Silent witnesses, shovels, and shards.
Beneath the weight of snowy shrouds,
Whispers echo, muffled clouds.

A world transformed, serene and bright,
Where shadows dance in pale moonlight.
With every gust, a breath of peace,
In whispered secrets that never cease.

Through crystal air, the stillness calls,
As winter's grasp around us falls.
The secrets linger, soft and pure,
In whispers of the frost's allure.

Shivering Expressions of Solitude

Lonely paths under starlit skies,
Shivering breaths, where silence lies.
Frosted air, a cold caress,
In solitude, we find our mess.

Windswept thoughts, a quiet din,
In every heart, the chill begins.
Echoes of laughter, far away,
In the winter, shadows play.

Bare branches reach for warmth and light,
In the depths of the endless night.
Chilled to the bone, yet thoughts run deep,
In solitude, awake we weep.

Each flake that falls bears witness true,
To moments spent in shades of blue.
A blend of pain and peace entwined,
In shivering hearts, solace we find.

Yet here we stand, in frigid grace,
Hiding behind a frozen face.
In every breath, a story told,
Of shivering warmth in bitter cold.

Frosted Dreams on Winter's Breath

In twilight's glow, with frosted breath,
Where dreams emerge from icy death.
Each whisper holds a tale to share,
As snowflakes dance in winter air.

Luminous nights where shadows sleep,
Awakening dreams, the heart does keep.
Within the frost, a gentle plea,
For warmth and light, for us to see.

Chasing visions through the cold,
In enchanted realms, we're bold.
Frosted paths lead where we dare,
To find our hopes amid despair.

A canvas white with futures bright,
Within the chill, we seek the light.
With every breath, we weave and spin,
Frosted dreams whispering within.

Nature's chill, a tender kiss,
In every moment, fleeting bliss.
We close our eyes and feel the freeze,
As winter's breath brings us to ease.

Silent Overture of the Ice

Beneath the still, a symphony plays,
In perfect quiet, where sunlight strays.
Each crack and creak, a note sublime,
A silent overture of time.

The icy lake, a mirror bright,
Reflects the stars that grace the night.
Shimmering shards in moonlit splendor,
An orchestra of winter's tender.

Snowflakes fall like whispered tunes,
Woven gently by the moon's runes.
In frozen beauty, hearts align,
As we embrace this song divine.

With every gust, a harmony stirs,
In the breath of ice, the music purrs.
In silent spaces, deep and wide,
The overture of winter's pride.

Each frozen sigh, a tale to keep,
In the arms of night, where shadows creep.
As blossoms fade and seasons turn,
The silent hymn of frost we yearn.

The Language of Silent Snow

Whispers fall from skies of gray,
Silent flurries float and sway,
Each flake tells a tale untold,
In winter's hush, the world turns cold.

Soft blankets cover all in white,
Footsteps vanish, lost from sight,
The trees stand tall, adorned in lace,
In the stillness, time finds grace.

Through the woods, the shadows creep,
While dreams of warmth begin to seep,
A tranquil heart in nature's rest,
In snowy whispers, we are blessed.

As twilight paints the deepening hue,
The moonlight casts a silver view,
In the silence, secrets flow,
This is the language of snow.

Deep in the night, cold breezes hum,
Echoes of winter softly drum,
In every drift, in every sigh,
The world wraps in a lullaby.

Breath of a Winter's Night

The stars like diamonds twinkle bright,
In the breath of a winter's night,
Each puff of air a frosty kiss,
As shadows dance in the gentle mist.

Silent whispers through the trees,
Carried softly on the breeze,
A blanket of calm, all else is still,
In the heart of night, a peaceful thrill.

The moon a guardian, shining white,
Illuminates the quiet night,
Where dreams emerge, and hopes take flight,
In the embrace of the winter light.

Footsteps on the crunching snow,
A tapestry of night aglow,
Each sound a story, old yet new,
In winter's breath, the world feels true.

The cold wraps round like a soft caress,
In winter's night, we find our rest,
For in its chill, there lies a warmth,
A tender peace, to which we swarth.

Sibilant Frost on the Breeze

A shimmer crowns the sleeping ground,
In frosty breath, there's magic found,
Sibilant whispers fill the air,
A winter's secret, soft and rare.

The night unfolds with icy grace,
Each flake a dancer, takes its place,
In the quiet, nature sings,
Of frost and snow, of gentle things.

Moonlight glistens on the trees,
Where frozen laughter rides the breeze,
The world adorned in crystalline,
A dreamscape born of cold divine.

Beneath the stars, we softly tread,
Through frosted realms where footsteps spread,
Time drifts slow, in blissful ease,
Amongst the sibilant sounds of freeze.

In every breath, the cold enchants,
With whispers of old, the heart recants,
A tranquil pause, a fleeting tease,
In winter's grasp, we've found our keys.

Murmurs Found in the Ice

In crystal caves where silence dwells,
Murmurs rise like hidden spells,
The icy breath of time stands still,
In nature's grasp, a magic thrill.

As winter weaves its frosty thread,
Stories dance, both heard and read,
In every glimmer, secrets lie,
In frozen breath, the echoes sigh.

Among the shards of sparkling white,
Ghostly whispers take their flight,
In the cold embrace, we find our place,
Wrapped in winter's silent grace.

Each step we take, the world can hear,
Murmurs loud, yet crystal clear,
In the ice, the heart does speak,
Of all the things we dare to seek.

So let us walk through winter's sheen,
Where frozen dreams can be seen,
In nature's hush, the truths unfold,
Murmurs found in the ice, so bold.

Veils of Silence

In shadows deep, whispers roam,
Softly treading, far from home.
Wrapped in night, secrets speak,
Veils of silence, so mystique.

Echoes dance through tranquil air,
Hung like dreams, beyond all care.
A heart that beats with wordless grace,
In the quiet, we find our place.

Fleeting thoughts upon the breeze,
Invisible threads, found with ease.
Moments linger, softly spun,
In the stillness, we become one.

With every sigh, a story told,
In the hush, life's beauty unfolds.
Weaving magic, soft and light,
Veils of silence, pure delight.

Glimmers of Frost

Beneath the moon's soft glow tonight,
Glimmers of frost, a pure delight.
Each crystal spark, a fleeting kiss,
In winter's embrace, a tranquil bliss.

Silent trees in silver dress,
Whispering tales of quietness.
As stars twinkle, sharp and bright,
Frosty wonders fill the night.

Footprints trace a fragile line,
Moments lost in winter's shine.
Nature's canvas, painted white,
Glimmers of frost, a breath of light.

Frozen whispers, soft and low,
Time stands still in moonlit glow.
Underneath the vast expanse,
Glimmers of frost invite a dance.

Crystal Conversations

In the quiet, voices blend,
Words like diamonds, softly send.
Crystal thoughts in the air,
Conversations, light as prayer.

Every glance a story penned,
Fragments of time, we comprehend.
Laughter twirls like dappled light,
In this moment, hearts take flight.

Subtle whispers, woven near,
Secrets shared without a fear.
Infinity found in a glance,
Crystal conversations, a sweet chance.

We dance through memories, bright and clear,
Echoes of joy, laughter's cheer.
In the spaces between us, true,
Crystal conversations, me and you.

Midnight's Frosted Serenade

Under stars, a world reborn,
Midnight's frost, a song is worn.
Notes like petals, drifting free,
In the dark, a symphony.

Glistening dreams on chilly air,
Whispers weave, a gentle care.
Each breath taken, crisp and clear,
In the night, we draw near.

The moon hums softly, guiding light,
In frozen grace, we find our sight.
Melodies wrapped in silver lace,
Midnight's serenade, a sweet embrace.

Hearts in rhythm, beating true,
Songs of winter, made anew.
In the silence, echoes play,
Midnight's frosted serenade.

Frosted Dreams

In the quiet of the night,
Snowflakes gently fall,
Whispers of a dream,
Blanket the world small.

Footprints left behind,
Tell tales of fading light,
While the stars above,
Glisten with pure delight.

Branches draped in white,
Sparkle in the moon's glow,
Each breath a frosty puff,
Set adrift in the flow.

The winds hum softly now,
Carrying secrets old,
Of wishes trapped in time,
And stories yet untold.

Frosted dreams will linger,
In the heart of winter's night,
With each ethereal sigh,
A world wrapped up in white.

Echoes of Ice

Beneath the frozen sky,
Echoes dance and twirl,
Shimmering reflections,
Of a capricious world.

Crystals form and melt,
In patterns ever bright,
Chasing fleeting shadows,
Through the soft, cold light.

The frozen streams do whisper,
Tales of days gone by,
Silent melodies flow,
Underneath the sky.

As winds weave through the trees,
And laughter fills the air,
Nature plays its symphony,
In this crystal affair.

Each echo tells a story,
Of hope amidst the chill,
In this icy realm we wander,
With hearts and dreams to fill.

Beneath a Shimmering Veil

Stars glimmer on the snow,
A soft, enchanting show,
Nature wraps her beauty,
In a graceful, silken glow.

Beneath the shimmering veil,
Of frost and winter charm,
Every breath a secret,
Every touch a warm balm.

Whispers trace the mountains,
In a language all its own,
A canvas painted white,
Where magic has been sown.

The silence sings a song,
Of dreams that take their flight,
While the world sleeps on,
Embraced by soft moonlight.

In this serene stillness,
Hearts find their gentle peace,
Underneath a shimmering veil,
Where all worries cease.

Whispers of the Winter Moon

Underneath the pale moon,
Whispers float on the breeze,
Echoes of ancient stories,
Told among the trees.

The night sky bathes the world,
In a soft and silver hue,
While starlight holds its breath,
In a realm known by few.

Frost adorns each window,
Like lace from a bygone day,
Capturing the moments,
That quietly slip away.

As shadows gently dance,
The earth is dressed in white,
Every step a whisper,
In the stillness of the night.

With every gentle sigh,
The winter moon will share,
The secrets of the cold,
Wrapped in frosty air.

Quivering Notes of Winter

In frosty air, the whispers glide,
Soft melodies, where shadows bide.
Each flake falls gently, a silent tune,
Under the gaze of a glowing moon.

Branches bow as chill winds play,
A symphony of night and day.
Crystals dance on the frozen stream,
Nature's song, a pastel dream.

The silence echoes, crisp and bright,
Winter's breath, a magical sight.
Harmony wraps the world so tight,
In quivering notes of purest white.

Footsteps crunch through the silent maze,
Each sound a echo, a winter praise.
Hidden realms in the snowy depth,
Winter's breath, a quiet theft.

So let us listen, hearts in flight,
To quivering notes that spark delight.
In every flake, a story told,
In winter's grasp, our dreams unfold.

Reverberations of the Icy Night

Stars above flicker in the void,
A canvas dark, mysteries deployed.
Moonlight weaves through the frigid trees,
In an icy embrace, we find our ease.

The air is thick with shimmering ice,
Each heartbeat thrums, a quiet slice.
Footsteps resonate on the frozen ground,
In this stillness, a pulse is found.

Whispers of winds carry tales untold,
Of ancient secrets and winters bold.
Nighttime descends with a velvet touch,
Cradling frost that means so much.

Echoes linger in the starry expanse,
A nocturnal rhythm, a solemn dance.
The world wrapped up in silvered threads,
With every sigh, a wish that spreads.

Graceful shadows move, soft and light,
In the heart of the reverberating night.
A brilliance found in the chill's embrace,
In icy realms, we find our place.

The Quiet Storm of Winter's Beauty

Gentle winds whisp through the pines,
A quiet storm, where nature shines.
Snowflakes swirl in a graceful spin,
As winter's beauty begins within.

Branches heavy with soft white glow,
A tranquil vision, a peaceful flow.
Frost-kissed landscapes stretch far and wide,
In the heart of winter, we abide.

The world transforms in nodding silence,
An ethereal dance, poised with elegance.
Each breath is visible, crisp and clear,
As winter's beauty draws us near.

Lakes stand still, a glassy dream,
Reflecting skies in a silver beam.
As daylight fades, the night is drawn,
In the quiet storm, our fears are gone.

Softly now, let the magic stir,
In winter's charm, both deep and pure.
Wrapped in whispers, we find our way,
In the quiet storm of the winter day.

Songs of the Frigid Universe

In the depths where starlight fades,
Songs are woven in icy braids.
Galaxies hum with a chill so bright,
Echoes weaving through endless night.

Frozen whispers float on the breeze,
Carried far over snow-cloaked trees.
Celestial harmonies spill and swirl,
As the universe in beauty unfurls.

Night ignites with a peaceful grace,
In the cosmic embrace, we find our place.
Each shimmering star, a note so clear,
In the vastness, winter's cheer.

Melodies mingle in planetary streams,
Crystalline echoes of timeless dreams.
In the silence, a vibrant song,
Of the frigid universe, where we belong.

Listen close, let your spirit soar,
In the symphony of forevermore.
As we dance on the edge of time,
In the icy songs, we find our rhyme.

Muffled Traces

Footsteps fade in the snow,
Whispers buried deep below.
Shadows linger, time stands still,
Stories hush, the world to kill.

Fragments of a memory lost,
Haunting echoes at what cost.
In the silence, secrets creep,
Muffled traces, dreams to keep.

Through the twilight, they unveil,
Ghostly paths in a silent trail.
A fleeting touch of what once was,
Muffled traces, nature's pause.

Beneath the frost, a heartbeat stirs,
Embers glow in quiet purrs.
Each step taken, night draws near,
Muffled traces, crystal clear.

In the stillness of the night,
Stars above hold tight their light.
A journey ends, a new one starts,
Muffled traces in our hearts.

Frosting on the Dawn

Morning breaks with gentle grace,
Whispers of a soft embrace.
Glistening on the fields of white,
Frosting dreams in pale twilight.

The world adorned in icy lace,
Nature's art, a fleeting trace.
Birdsong dances in the air,
Frosting on the dawn, so fair.

Silhouettes of trees outlined,
A whispered promise, intertwined.
Radiance of the golden sun,
Frosting tells of night undone.

Moments pause as shadows play,
Colors blend where night meets day.
A canvas kissed by winter's breath,
Frosting's touch, a dance with death.

As the chill begins to fade,
Hope emerges, softly laid.
A world awakes, reborn anew,
Frosting on the dawn, in hue.

The Secret Language of Ice

Crystals form in spectral dance,
Nature's whispers, a fleeting chance.
Secrets held in frozen sighs,
The silent truth that never lies.

Beneath the surface, stories weave,
In frozen layers, we believe.
Words unspoken, knowledge glows,
The secret language, nature knows.

With every crack, a tale is spun,
A history of what's begun.
The chill of winter speaks so clear,
The secret language, drawing near.

Frosted windows capture light,
Moments pause in ghostly flight.
Listen closely, for hearts entice,
In the stillness, the language of ice.

As winters change to spring's embrace,
The whispers fade, yet leave a trace.
Forever etched in time's sort,
The secret language, nature's court.

Chilled Echoes

Winds of winter softly ride,
Chilled echoes, time does abide.
In the silence, voices rise,
Haunting memories in disguise.

Echoes through the frosty air,
Whispers lost in burdens bare.
Footsteps dancing, shadows blend,
Chilled echoes that never end.

Through the twilight, stories flow,
In the frost, they gently glow.
Silent echoes, softly speak,
In the quiet, hearts grow weak.

Lurking doubts and dreams once clear,
In chilled echoes, doubt draws near.
Voices beckon, soft and low,
Chilled echoes in the snow.

But within the cold, a fire burns,
In every echo, life returns.
Hope is found in every trace,
Chilled echoes, a warm embrace.

Fragments of Frozen Light

In the dawn's soft glow, they break,
Whispers of ice on the lake,
Flickers of stars in the night,
Chasing the shadows of fright.

Crystals dance in the breeze,
With every sigh, nature frees,
Moments caught in a breath,
Echoes of life and of death.

As daylight fades to dusk,
Colors blend, a gentle musk,
Nature's tapestry on display,
A fleeting memory of day.

In silence, the fragments gleam,
A tapestry, more than a dream,
Every shard tells a tale,
Of night and the morning pale.

Hold close these moments bright,
In the depths of the night,
For time is but a fragile thread,
Woven through words unsaid.

Subtle Murmurs in the Cold

Whispers float on the frosty air,
Echoes of things we cannot share,
Sigh of the wind through the trees,
Conversations carried with ease.

Crimson leaves fall and twirl,
Silent confessions in a whirl,
Nature speaks in hushed tones,
Tales of heart and of bones.

Underneath the starlit sky,
Softly the world breathes a sigh,
Each breath a moment, a spark,
Fleeting as light in the dark.

As frost kisses ground and stone,
We find warmth in the unknown,
Every murmur a hidden grace,
A quiet kiss from this place.

In the stillness, find your voice,
Embrace the calm, make your choice,
For in each whisper, we learn,
The beauty of the seasons turn.

Shards of Winter's Lament

Cascading flakes, a fragile fall,
In the chill, we hear their call,
Melodies of silence prevail,
In the twilight, we set sail.

Each shard a story for the eyes,
Underneath the somber skies,
Gathering warmth from the cold,
Tales of winter yet untold.

Breath of the night, crisp and clear,
Echoes of laughter, far and near,
Time drifts softly in the air,
To the rhythm of despair.

Carved in frost upon the ground,
A symphony without a sound,
Listen close, and you might hear,
Winter's sigh, so raw, so near.

Yet in the chilling embrace,
A softness, a gentle grace,
For even winter understands,
The warmth of love in frozen lands.

Ethereal Caress of Hail

A sudden hush, then a storm,
In the air, an electric form,
Murmurs rise with the swell,
As nature's magic casts its spell.

Each drop a note from the skies,
Bursting forth with soft goodbyes,
A dance of light on the ground,
In this chaos, beauty found.

Within the tempest, secrets swell,
Whispers of life sing and dwell,
Crystals fall, a fleeting kiss,
Moments made of blissful mist.

Every hailstone's gentle touch,
Carries stories, oh so much,
A tapestry, wild and wild,
In nature's tears, we are a child.

So let the heavens pour their grace,
In every storm, a warm embrace,
For even hail, with its might,
Carries a promise of light.

Shimmering Whispers

Underneath the silver moon,
Softly dance the stars in tune.
Whispers carried on the breeze,
Telling tales among the trees.

Gentle light begins to play,
Painting shadows, night and day.
In the hush, a magic hum,
Nature's heart begins to drum.

Every glimmer, every spark,
Echoes in the deepening dark.
Lost in dreams, we softly glide,
Where shimmering secrets reside.

A symphony of sounds unfold,
Stories of the night retold.
In the silence, wisdom reigns,
Whispers lost in moonlit plains.

With each breath, a promise made,
In the night's embrace, we wade.
Shimmering whispers, soft and bright,
Guide us through this starry night.

Earth in Hibernation

Beneath a blanket, quiet, deep,
Nature rests, in peace it sleeps.
The world outside, a silent gray,
In hibernation, slowing day.

Mountains cloaked in snowy white,
Stars above, a dazzling sight.
Frozen lakes reflect the sky,
While gentle winds whisper by.

Roots secure in frosty ground,
In this stillness, life is found.
Dreams are woven in the cold,
Hidden stories yet untold.

Patience wrapped in winter's heart,
Waiting for the spring's new start.
Each day passes, slow and sweet,
As life prepares to stand on feet.

The earth will wake, the buds will bloom,
Life returns to dispel the gloom.
In hibernation, secrets lie,
Awaiting warmth from the sky.

Echoes of a Frozen Dream

In the stillness of the night,
Echoes drift, so soft and light.
Frozen whispers on the air,
Carried visions, dreams laid bare.

Icicles like crystal tears,
Hold the memory of our fears.
In the silence, shadows creep,
Guarding secrets we must keep.

Snowflakes dance, a fleeting waltz,
Painting landscapes without faults.
Every flake a story spun,
In this world, we are but one.

Echoes linger, soft and true,
Dreams entwined in silver blue.
With each breath, a past we share,
In frozen dreams, we linger there.

As dawn breaks with golden rays,
Promises born from icy days.
Echoes fade, a soft goodbye,
While new dreams take to the sky.

The Breath of Winter's Night

From the depths of night, a sigh,
Winter's breath as stars pass by.
Chill and calm, a tranquil scene,
In the dark, the world serene.

Frosted air, a crystal bite,
Holding whispers of the night.
Moonlight blankets all below,
Wrapped in silence, soft and slow.

Branches bare, the trees stand tall,
Echoing the night's sweet call.
Every moment feels so near,
In this breath, we shed our fear.

Snowflakes swirl in graceful flight,
Painting dreams in purest white.
Nature rests, no need to fight,
Lost within winter's quiet night.

With each breath, a story flows,
Tales of warmth 'neath icy shows.
In winter's grasp, our hearts take flight,
Embraced by the breath of night.

A Dance on the Frost

In the crisp air, we twirl and spin,
Footprints glisten, where we've been.
Under the moon, shadows gleam,
Nature joins our joyous dream.

The trees stand tall, draped in white,
Whispers of magic fill the night.
With every step, the world holds still,
Hearts entwined, we chase the thrill.

The stars above, a celestial show,
Guiding our dance through the frosty glow.
Laughter floats, a sweet refrain,
In this moment, we feel no pain.

The chill wraps round, but we don't mind,
In this embrace, warmth we find.
A dance on frost, a timeless art,
Two souls united, heart to heart.

Whispered Lullabies

Under the stars, soft breezes sigh,
Moonlit whispers, lullabies fly.
Gentle caress of night's embrace,
Dreams unspool in this sacred space.

Crickets hum their sweet refrain,
Murmurs of love linger in the plain.
The world fades in a tender sigh,
As shadows cradle the slumbering sky.

Floating notes like feathers divine,
Woven together, yours and mine.
Holding close, as time slows down,
In whispered tunes, no trace of the crown.

Echoes of warmth in the cool night air,
Every heartbeat, a promise to share.
In this slumber, where dreams reside,
Whispered lullabies, our hearts abide.

Snowflakes' Secret

Gently falling from the sky,
Snowflakes whisper as they sigh.
Each one unique, a silent art,
Holding nature's secret, pure heart.

They dance and swirl on winter's breath,
A fleeting life before their death.
Every flake, a story untold,
In their softness, wonders unfold.

Beneath the frost, a world asleep,
Winter's magic, soft and deep.
Yet in each flake, a sparkle bright,
Reminds us of warmth in the night.

Together, they blanket the earth,
In their elegance, they whisper worth.
Snowflakes' secret, a transient kiss,
Nature's discussion, a moment of bliss.

The Frozen Heartbeat

In the stillness of the cold,
Heartbeat whispers, tales unfold.
Frozen pulses beneath the snow,
Echoes of feelings that softly flow.

Winter's breath caresses the night,
Shadows mingle, a tender sight.
Amidst the chill, warmth does ignite,
The frozen heartbeat, love's own light.

Silent promises, we hold so dear,
In every hush, the world draws near.
Crystals sparkle, a frozen dream,
In silence, our hearts learn to beam.

Together we tread on this icy ground,
Where hope and longing can be found.
The frozen heartbeat sings so sweet,
In winter's embrace, our souls compete.

Milton Keynes UK
Ingram Content Group UK Ltd.
UKHW010229111224
452348UK00011B/610